MLM'S

DIRTY
LITTLE
SECRETS

AN INSIDERS
LOOK BEHIND
THE CURTAINS

JOHN MALOTT

MLM'S DIRTY LITTLE SECRETS! AN INSIDERS LOOK BEHIND THE CURTAIN!

Why? I was once told by the late great Paul J Meyer "know your reason Why? Once you know why to do something, you will figure out how to do that thing. The why is more important than the how."

So, let's start with why listen to me? Let's face it, I'm not a writer. Hell, I had to google what a "prologue" is! My spelling sucks so bad even spell check gave up! Grammar, paragraph breaks and punctuation, definitely not my strong suit. I finger peck out approximately 5 words per minute, and I accidentally deleted half this book after I wrote it! UGHH.

I've also failed more times than I care to admit. I've been labeled a loser, reject, dropout, and failure. I don't always say the right things. I won't always tell you what you want to hear, but I will tell you the truth. I've picked up my share of haters, in and outside of this profession.

I already know some network marketing "leaders" will be discouraging "their people" from reading this book. Jealousy and ego are interesting animals.

Here is some of what I am. I'm an entrepreneur, a builder, an action taker, a leader, a father, a husband and a loyal friend. I'm passionate and purpose driven. I'm a bit of an empath. I'm extremely protective of the people I care about. I'd throat punch you in a second if you harmed my wife or kids. I'm Loyal, maybe to a fault (if that's even possible). I'm afraid to live in poverty again. My work ethic is second to none.

I've worked for over 2 decades on and in this profession. Logged countless miles by car and air. Put in long hours and sleepless nights. Put my credit card on the line to secure rooms for events so many times even my accountant had trouble understanding. I've laughed, cried, shared so many successes and failures with distributers its mind boggling. I gave even when I didn't have it to give.

Why this book? Because our profession needs a voice. Needs someone to defend it and call it out. To speak up, to admit we have some problems. To offer solutions. To be transparent. To be relevant and unafraid. This little book is a guide, a beacon and a clarion call to action.

This book should of course be shared with everyone in our profession. Share it with your leadership and your organization. I also believe we should share it with our haters. I expose a bunch of the lies and myths that haters tend to use as fuel to spew their fire.

This book should have you take a deep look inside yourself. Force you to ask some tough questions. Ultimately this book is about taking responsibility. One hundred percent responsibility for everything, everything!

Our profession has a publicity problem. Ultimately, the future of it lands squarely in our hands, the promoters of it, you, and I!

Why you? Because as my friend Les Brown would say "You have greatness within you".

The world is throwing a lot at you right now. The media especially social media has us questioning ourselves, comparing ourselves to people we never met, sometimes depressed and stressed. Never satisfied, never enough.

You can live to your potential. Use this to keep you between the rails, on course, moving swiftly and steadily towards your goals.

Enjoy the journey.
John Malott

CONTENTS

INTRODUCTION

WE HAVE BEEN BAMBOOZLED, HOODWINKED, I TELL YOU!

My name is John Malott, but my name is not as important as what I do and what I'm about to share with you. I'm widely considered the #1 home-based business expert. I'm also known as the Anti-MLM Network marketer. You will rarely find me hanging with your favorite MLM guru, you won't find me writing blogs about the profession, and you'll almost never find me on the popular network marketing stages. Not that I'm against it. It's just that the truth isn't always what's on their menus. When I am invited, it's because they (A) know my name will sell more tickets or (B) are truly interested in impact over BS.

Over the past twenty-plus years, I've been from the bottom making less than zero, to earning millions of dollars per year as an independent distributor, to founding, building, and leading my own network marketing company. I've also been working directly with top industry influencers, thought leaders, independent distributors, athletes, CEOs, and celebrities as a brand strategist. From traveling the world building large organizations to speaking on stages and guiding fellow entrepreneurs to reach seven figures and beyond, I've learned a lot about how to build, lead, and scale, and frankly—how **not** to!

Now, I don't have all the things that society says you are supposed to have to be successful. I don't have a college degree or even a high school diploma. So you're probably saying to yourself, "What is this clown going to teach me?" But before you check out, it's exactly who I was that forced me to look outside of the traditional employment and business routes. I'm convinced this is the reason I have enjoyed the massive success that I've had. My life depended on it!

In my career to date, my home-based network marketing organizations have grown to over three hundred thousand distributors in eight countries, and my companies have done combined sales of over $1.2 billion. I don't share that to brag, boast, or try to impress you, but rather to impress upon you that I know a thing or two about building a business from home.

Building an empire through network marketing is something that many try to do, and unfortunately, most get lost along the way. The failure stories are everywhere. We all have a relative, friend, or coworker who has a story or two about how they know someone who failed in MLM. So I started to look at why that is . . . Why do so many people start and give up before they really reap the benefits of their hard work? I phrase it that way because, really, the only way to fail is to quit.

CHAPTER 1

THE GOOD, BAD, AND UGLY

To understand the profession better, let's first look at some statistics:

1. Over twenty million Americans participate in MLM or have done so in the past.

According to facts about network marketing, a lot of Americans are already part of multi-level marketing. About 90% of them joined to make some money (Cision PR Newswire).

2. With $40.2 billion in direct sales, the US is the global MLM leader.

Based on MLM profit, the US reigns supreme. Coming in second, China generated $19.18 billion in the same period, followed by Germany with $17.97 billion. Next on the list are South Korea ($17.75 billion), Japan ($15.41 billion), Brazil ($8.25 billion), Malaysia ($6.98 billion), Mexico ($5.28 billion), France ($5.13 billion), and Taiwan ($4.46 billion) (Statista).

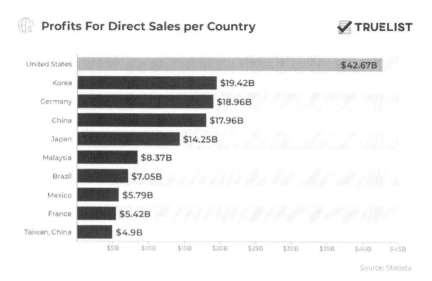

Profits For Direct Sales per Country   ✅ TRUELIST

Source: Statista

3. 75% of direct-selling participants in the US in 2020 were women.

Based on the data on MLM demographics for this segment in the US, women are predominantly involved in direct selling. Men, meanwhile, comprise only 25% of direct sellers (Statista).

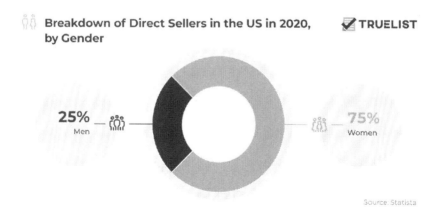

Breakdown of Direct Sellers in the US in 2020, by Gender   ✅ TRUELIST

25% Men

75% Women

Source: Statista

4. Around 75% of women participants in MLM have no experience in commission-based sales.

Not only are the majority of MLM sellers women, but most of them start with no experience in the industry. Education-wise, 66% of MLM participants were found to have attended college or graduated from it vs. 60% of those who have never had this type of job, multi-level marketing statistics show (AARP Foundation).

5. Roughly 2.7 million women in India work in network marketing and direct selling.

The network marketing industry seems to be characterized by strong female participation. The total involvement of women in India in the labor market is about 23.3%. MLM comprises 53% of the total women involved in the labor market in the country (Codeless).

6. In Europe, women comprise 84.9% of direct sellers.

MLM statistics suggest women are typically more involved in network marketing than men. In Europe, it's 84.9% vs. 15.1%. That's the largest percentage in favor of women. In the Americas, 80.2% of women are part of network marketing, as opposed to 19.8% of men. In Asia-Pacific, it's 68.5% vs. 31.5%, while in Africa and the Middle East, it's 63.8% vs. 36.2% (Epixel MLM Software).

7. The US is home to the top three most profitable MLMs, with joint revenue of about $19 billion.

Amway, with $8.8 billion in revenue; Avon, with $5.7 billion; and Herbalife, with $4.5 billion, are the top MLM companies, all located in the US. MLM statistics point to Mary Kay Europe and Vorwerk as the next top companies, which come from Germany and have revenue of $4.2 and $3.5 billion, respectively (Codeless).

DEXTER AND BIRDIE YAGER

Dexter and Birdie's story is one of humble beginnings, inclusiveness, and family bonding. They started their journey with Amway in 1964. Today, they have been Crown Ambassadors multiple times and their estimated annual income is $15.6 million. Their business spans across forty countries (Direct Selling Star).

How Big Is the Network Marketing Industry?

By 2025, the market is set to hit $237.63 billion, at a 6.5% CAGR. This growth is mostly credited to the expansion and recovery of companies following the COVID-19 impact (Globe Newswire).

> Clearly, the size and potential available market is not the problem. So let's dig deeper. Warning, here is where it starts to get ugly.

8. Herbalife had to pay $200 million in fines and restructure its business to solve charges from the FTC in the US.

The Federal Trade Commission fined Herbalife in 2016 due to misleading actions against consumers regarding their potential earnings. To comply, they had to reorganize their compensation plans. As a result, they reward actual product sales more than recruiting downline members (Family Finance Mom).

9. Advocare was fined $150 million by the FTC over false claims.

On top of that, the company had to stop working in the multi-level marketing business permanently due to false claims about offering a life-changing financial solution for individuals who want to earn unlimited income and quit their job (Family Finance Mom).

- At least 50% of MLM participants drop out after one year.

- 66% of MLM participants invest less than $1,000.

- Depending on the source, 1–25% of MLM participants turn a profit

So Let's Talk MLM Success Rates

So what are the success rates associated with MLMs? Unfortunately, only a small percentage of people make real money out of them. According to *Forbes* magazine, only 1–25% of participants actually succeed in turning a profit through their MLMs. This doesn't mean that no one makes money from MLMs—far from it—but most participants don't.

The challenge is in getting real data. Agendas on both sides make it convoluted and confusing at best, but here are some published stats on some of the most popular MLM companies:

- The pioneer of multilevel marketing (MLM), **Amway Corporation** manufactures and sells its own products as well as brand-name products from other companies through a network of **3 million** independent distributors worldwide.

- There are about 600,000 **Mary Kay** consultants in the United States.

- **MONAT Global Corp** has **more than 450,000** Market Partners.

- **My Daily Choice** has 60,000 affiliates.

- **O'Snap Active Lifestyle** has 4,000 brand Ambassadors.

- **LegalShield** has over 100,000 associates.

- **Herbalife** operates in ninety-five countries through a network of approximately **4.5 million** independent distributors and members.

CHAPTER 2

THOSE DAMN DISCLOSURE STATEMENTS

So the debate is now over who is active and who is not? Who is actually working and who is not? Income disclosure statements give the numbers, but do they really tell the story? Hardly.

Most companies today consider distributors that purchase a product or two *active*. They may also have some miniscule customer sales number for being considered active—we're usually talking a few hundred dollars max! That is hardly what would be considered active on a sales job or in any small business.

If you go back not that long ago, most joined the old-school pioneer companies like **Amway, Herbalife,** and **Mary Kay** as distributors in order to purchase products at "wholesale" prices. There really wasn't much differentiation between customer and distributor. This later proved to be problematic. On top of that, the people that maybe had the intent to distribute held demanding full-time jobs. The fact is even if they initially intended to "build the business," the demands of everyday life are relentless, to say the least. Building *any* business requires time, energy, and resources, not to mention training, skill development, and support. If the majority of distributors had less than $1,000 of skin in the game. How much rejection, energy, or work do you think it would take to knock them out of the game?

The original model led to massive challenges. Think about it. The naysayers have a field day with this. They love to point out the average incomes made in the company and how unlikely it will be to earn any income. They even go as far as to say it will take extreme luck to win in MLM. The commitment, skill set, work ethic, or activity of the individual distributor is rarely mentioned as a factor.

> To understand how they arrive at the doom-and-gloom failure statistics, let's examine a few income disclosure statements to see firsthand how terrible or not these companies really are.

Herbalife Income Disclosure Statement 2021:

There are no required purchases other than the initial Distributorship kit, also known as the International Business pack (IBP) ($125.50). • Distributors enjoy setting their own schedule and choosing how and when to work. • Most people start their Herbalife Nutrition business by working part-time and selling to people they know or people they meet as a way to make a little extra money. • There are no guarantees that you will earn money. Like all business people, some Distributors will succeed, while some will not. • Building a successful Herbalife Nutrition business takes skill, hard work, and time. How can I earn money? You can earn money by selling Herbalife Nutrition products that you buy at a discount. Your initial discount is approximately 25%. The more you sell, the higher your discount, up to a maximum of approximately 50%. For example, the initial discount on Formula 1, Herbalife Nutrition's best-selling product is shown on the right: • If you buy at this initial discount and sell 10 canisters at the Suggested Retail Price, passing along shipping and taxes, you would make $143.80 before expenses. • You can also earn money from the sales of people you sponsor. • You cannot earn money by only recruiting or only sponsoring someone. In addition to retail earnings, how much could I earn from sales by Distributors I sponsor? In addition to any retail profit, of those Distributors with at least 1 (one) complete year of tenure (17% or 3,750) who received earnings from Herbalife Nutrition on sales by Distributors they sponsored, before expenses: Distributors 1 Year + (3,750) 50% (about 1,875) earned more than $444. Top 10% (about 375) earned more than $5,662. Top 1% (about 38) earned more than $118,762. In 2021, the tenure of the top 1% Distributors ranged from 3 to 39 years.

Amway Income Disclosure Statement 2021:

In 2021, 33% of all Amway US registered IBOs had no reported sales, did not sponsor another IBO, and did not earn any compensation from Amway; 62% of all US registered IBOs in 2021 received a payment from Amway in at least one month for sales that occurred during 2021. Of the IBOs who received a payment from Amway in one or more months, here is what they annually earned before expenses: • The Top

1% earned $87,901 (average) and $55,264 (median) • The Top 10% earned $14,537 (average) and $4,645 (median) • The Top 50% earned $3,414 (average) and $631 (median).

MONAT USA 2021 Income Disclosure Statement:

The average annual income for ALL US Market Partners at all ranks (which includes Active and Inactive Market Partners) in 2021 was $ 831. Thirty-nine percent of US Market Partners were not Active in 2021 and therefore did not earn any commissions. The income information in the chart below includes Active and Inactive Market Partners in 2021. An "Active" Market Partner is a Market Partner who earned any amount of commissions in the 2021 calendar year. An "Inactive" Market Partner is a Market Partner who did not earn any amount of commissions in the 2021 calendar year. A Market Partner's Rank may vary over the course of a year, for purposes of the chart below, the Rank of each MONAT Market Partner is the Highest Achieved Title that the Market Partner achieved for at least three months within the 2021 calendar year. Those enrolled in November and December 2021 the Highest Achieved Title was used for the Highest Achieved for two months.

High Annual Gross Earnings ranged from $21,889 to $3,531,73

Low Annual Gross Earnings $ 0 $ 379,433

Median Annual Gross Earnings $ 21 $ 1,106,283

Median No. of Months to Achieve Rank 2 to 24 months

Income Depending on time and rank

Modere 2019 Income Disclosure Statement:

All income is earned on the sale of Modere products. No benefits or bonuses are paid or received solely through recruiting or enrolling other Social Marketers, and no earnings are guaranteed from mere participation in the Compensation Plan.

Commission Earned Ranges	Monthly Average Commissions[1]	Percent of Active Social Marketers[2]	Percent of Total Commission Earners[3]
$0.01-200	$53.60	22.10%	64.51%
$201-500	$350.47	6.02%	17.56%
$501-2,000	$1,121.04	3.50%	10.21%
$2,001-5,000	$3,375.61	1.77%	5.15%
$5,001-10,000	$7,854.48	0.33%	0.97%
$10,001-20,000	$13,618.54	0.29%	0.84%
$20,001-50,000	$31,395.33	0.16%	0.48%
$50,000+	$106,291.25	0.10%	0.28%

MY Daily Choice Income Disclosure Statement 2021:

Compensation

- Retail Profits on products sold to Customers: Independent Affiliates have the option to resell MDC products from wholesale purchases for retail prices and keep the difference.

- Commissions from the MDC Compensation Plan: The MDC Compensation Plan offers multiple options to receive bonuses and commissions based on the product sales from an Independent Affiliate and their team. Commissions and bonuses cannot be earned by simply recruiting others to join.

Rank	Average Annual	Lowest Earned Monthly	Highest Earned Monthly
Builder	$78.24	$0.50	$7,658.62
Director	$94.92	$0.30	$7,942.62
Executive	$395.64	$1.20	$19,021.24
1K	$5,977.32	$1.20	$19,567.68
5K	$16,021.08	$29.50	$25,919.41
10K	$33,426.00	$461.36	$34,804.50
25K	$71,209.92	$517.40	$35,110.29
50K	$142,204.56	$2,557.15	$78,722.52
100K	$261,400.68	$6,364.56	$80,832.26
250K	$609,345.00	$12,615.46	$102,082.15
500K	$902,876.28	$19,116.20	$162,953.87
SUPER	$2,362,677.72	$115,310.66	$489,043.20

Typical Earnings

The average annual income for all Affiliates (22,338) who sponsored at least one person and had some activity in 2021 was $1,511.50 and about 29% (6,397) received no income at all.

- Approximately 63% of Independent Affiliates earned less than $100.00 in 2021.

- The average income for the top 10% (2,233) was $9,502.34

- The average income for the top 2% (446) was $35,654.62. The average time for the top 2% of earners to get there was approximately 13 months.

These figures do not include any expenses an Affiliate incurred to operate their business. These figures should not be construed as guarantees or projections of actual earnings or profits. Success with MyDailyChoice results only from successful sales efforts, which require hard work, diligence and leadership.

Refund Policy

MDC offers a full refund less shipping for products that are returned within the timeline listed in the Refund Policies on the company website. If an Affiliate decides the business is not for them and resigns, they can return all unopened and resalable products for a 90% refund less any shipping fees.

CHAPTER 3

NETWORK MARKETING VS. GLOBAL DISTRIBUTION OF WEALTH

The latest available data from the EPI shows that in 2020 annual wages for the top 1% reached $823,763, up 7.3% compared to 2019. How much do you need to earn to be in the top 0.1%? A hefty $3,212,486, which is almost 10% more than that group earned a year before. Wages for the bottom 90% rose at a much more modest rate of just 1.7% over the same period, with an average income of $40,085.[1]

The US has more billionaires than any other country: 735. China, including Hong Kong and Macao, is close behind with 607. Highlighting a racial wealth gap, only eight of America's billionaires are African American: businessmen Robert F. Smith and David Steward, Oprah Winfrey, Kanye West, Rihanna, Michael Jordan, Jay-Z, and Tyler Perry.[2]

1   Economic Policy Institute https://www.epi.org/blog/wage-inequality-continued-to-increase-in-2020-top-1-0-of-earners-see-wages-up-179-since-1979-while-share-of-wages-for-bottom-90-hits-new-low/.

2   https://www.forbes.com/billionaires/

2020 Average Annual Wages[3]

Group	Avg. Wages
Top 0.1% of Earners	$3,212,486
Top 1% of Earners	$823,763
Top 5% of Earners	$342,987
Top 10% of Earners	$173,176

In 2021, the bottom 90% of workers earned only **58.6%** of total earnings, while the top 5% earned 29.9%. That is, a group of workers that is eighteen times as big in size earned only about twice as much as the much smaller group.[4]

In 2021 an estimated **698 million people**, or 9% of the global population, are living in extreme poverty—that is, living on less than $1.90 a day.[5]

Income disparity is a real thing. But critics use MLM's part-time, sometime, sign up and choose to do nothing, volunteer workforce as an easy target.

---

3   Julia Kagan, Investopedia, Updated September 17, 2022.

4   https://www.epi.org/publication/inequality-2021-ssa-data/

5   https://www.worldvision.org/sponsorship-news-stories/global-poverty-facts

> **Let's take a peek behind the scenes of the United States of America. I'm sure the income numbers of the richest country on the planet are fair and equitable, right?**

In 2021, about **37.93 million** people were living below the poverty line in the United States, an increase from the previous year.[6]

Millions of people in the USA would effectively have zero income if not for our government entitlement programs.

Let that sink in!

I found it interesting that right in the income disclosure statements of many established network marketing companies they have earners that easily fall into the top 0.1% of wage earners category.

The fact that it's clearly not just possible, not just in one company, but companies all over the network marketing profession. IT HAS ACTUALLY BEEN DONE! This should be enough for some to say "if another man or woman can do it surely I can do it".

I am still looking for a network marketing company with the entitlement compensation plan.

---

6   https://www.census.gov/library/publications/2022/demo/p60-277.html

CHAPTER 4

MENACE TO SOCIETY

This chapter really hits home for me. My first felony arrest was when I was fifteen years old. My second and last were when I was twenty-four.

Let me share some numbers that should scare the shit out of us all. Formerly incarcerated people have little chance of finding and maintaining gainful employment.

Post-release, months of searching, and moving between jobs are common. The overall employment rate over four years after the study population was released hovered between **34.9% and 37.9%**—in other words, about two-thirds of the population were jobless at any given time. This is definitely not good.

How many formerly incarcerated people are jobless at the moment? A good guess would be 60%, to generalize from a new report released by the Bureau of Justice Statistics (BJS)[7]. The report shows that of more

---

than fifty thousand people released from federal prisons in 2010, a staggering 33% found no employment at all over four years post-release, and at any given time, no more than 40% of the cohort was employed. People who did find jobs struggled too: Formerly incarcerated people in the sample had an average of 3.4 jobs throughout the four-year study period, suggesting that they were landing jobs that didn't offer security or upward mobility.

Newly released data doubles down on what we've reported before: Formerly incarcerated people face huge obstacles to finding stable employment, leading to detrimental society-wide effects. Considering the current labor market, there may be plenty of jobs available, but they don't guarantee stability or economic mobility for this vulnerable population.

As the new data shows, one way or another, formerly incarcerated people have been routinely shut out of the workforce and denied access to opportunity. Criminal legal system involvement only makes their chances of finding a job worse, and these economic losses compound over time, making communities hit hardest by mass incarceration even worse off.[8]

We tend to not think of this type of thing as a me problem. Yet we all have a friend or a relative or someone not too far removed from our circle that we know dealing with this or have been a victim of. Maybe it's a cousin, brother, sister, son, or daughter.

I don't have all the answers here, but I will tell you the current system is not working! I can tell you firsthand what it's like to have doors shut

8   Leah Wang and Wanda Bertram, February 8, 2022 prisonpolicy.org.

in your face, opportunities stripped away because of mistakes made but paid for in the past. What do you think desperate people are going to do? There is no such thing as equal opportunity employment, but network marketing is the closest I've seen to a true equal opportunity, opportunity. When someone you know that has a "colorful" past tells you they are part of a network marketing company. Do them and society a favor. High five them and do everything you can to support and assist them. Last point on this. If you happen to be in a company and you never told them about it. Do not, I repeat DO NOT bash, look down on, attempt to recruit, discredit or criticize them or their company in any way. Look in the mirror! Don't make that mistake again. Be a pro, suck it up buttercup and move on.

> **"In Network Marketing work ethic and persistence beats talent every time. Develop an "I will not be denied" attitude and work until you have the life you envision for yourself!"**
>
> **-Joshua Denne**

CHAPTER 5

EDUCATED FAILURES

There is another part of this that very few understand: the skills one will learn along the way are priceless. If I never made a dime, what I became in the process was worth it. Where else would I have million-dollar producers pouring into me? I learned real-life skills that you can't put a price tag on. Here are some skills I learned: communication, leadership, team building, emotional intelligence, patience, sales, marketing, scaling, public speaking, resilience, technology, and finance, to name a few. These skills have made me valuable not only in the marketplace, but also to my family and society—and the cost was so miniscule (mainly time and small start-up cost).

Contrast that to the traditional education system, and something interesting emerges: the current educational system is clearly not working for most.

Millions of people go into serious debt for a college degree.

Here's a statistic that may give some pause: **More than half of college graduates over the age of twenty-five don't work in their field of study**, according to a new survey from Intelligent.com.[9]

How many people do you know don't work in the field they went to school for? The double whammy: How many people do you know don't work in their field of education yet still pay on student loans? Or do work in their field but are bogged down by student loans and average pay?

We still push this on our kids as the only way to success. Give me a break!

It's insane!

Go to college for networking, relationships, and the parties, not to be massively successful.

I know a lot of people in their late twenties, thirties, and even forties still paying on student loans! On top of that, I know very few that make six figures per year with their college degrees.

On the flip side, I know a lot of people enjoying six-figure passive income in network marketing. On top of that, they did not go into debt to do this.

School is big business, and we should evaluate it as such.

---

9   https://www.bloomberg.com/news/articles/2022-04-18/is-college-worth-it-most-graduates-work-in-other-fields

Imagine if we forced schools to produce income disclosure statements! We could form Reddit and Facebook fear-and-hate groups about how many failures and how much money these corrupt institutions are bilking out of these poor, unsuspecting, naive kids!

I was with a company, Pre-Paid Legal Services (today LegalShield), for over a decade. It's hard to understand how many associates there are earning six figures per year—and some seven figures. There are probably hundreds! However, the real untold story is the tens of thousands receiving checks every month from work they did years ago. The challenge and where the critics attempt to rip them apart is when they talk about how many "associates" have signed up and never gotten paid. They also never did anything to get paid, but that fact doesn't elicit fear and skepticism.

It's always fascinating to me what we perceive to be bad compared to what actually is bad.

"Consistency, focus and urgency are the three hallmarks of the careers of every six and seven figure earner in network marketing. It was because I embodied these three attributes that I out-earned so many people who were taller, better looking and had more outgoing personalities than me. When I wrote the book on exactly how we built a 400,000 person downline (Building an Empire, the best selling complete training guide in the industry), it's design was to give every single networker the precise blueprint to build a successful business. But here's the thing. I can give this book to one hundred people and only 3-5 of them will be urgent enough to read it and take action, with consistent focus on their business every day over an extended period of time. This is the very reason why some people make it to the top while most don't. The opportunity is equal, but these attributes in people are not. Can they be learned? For sure, but only if you put somebody with the right desire into an environment with the right associations and mentors.

Look at John Malott, watch him. You will see someone who is consistent, focused and urgently going after it. These are the kind of examples to model. You don't need to be like him, you just have to embody the attributes that make him successful. Become the best you, and decide you will become a top notch professional in this business arena. Success is a decision followed by daily choices."

-Brian Carruthers

CHAPTER 6

IMBALANCED EFFORT
AND RESULTS

Now, let's look at a widely accepted principle called the *Pareto principle* aka, the *80/20 rule*.[10] The Pareto principle states that for many outcomes, roughly 80% of consequences come from 20% of causes (the "vital few"). Other names for this principle are the *law of the vital few* or the *principle of factor sparsity*.

Management consultant Joseph M. Juran developed the concept in the context of quality control and improvement after reading the works of Italian sociologist and economist Vilfredo Pareto, who wrote about the 80/20 connection while teaching at the University of Lausanne. In his first work, *Cours d'économie politique*, Pareto showed that approximately 80% of the land in the Kingdom of Italy was owned by 20% of the population. The Pareto principle is only tangentially related to the Pareto efficiency.

Mathematically, the 80/20 rule is roughly described by a *power law distribution* (also known as a *Pareto distribution*) for a particular set of

10   https://en.wikipedia.org/wiki/Pareto_principle

parameters. Many natural phenomena distribute according to power law statistics. It is an adage of business management that "80% of sales come from 20% of clients."

In Economics

Pareto's observation was in connection with population and wealth. Pareto noticed that approximately 80% of Italy's land was owned by 20% of the population. He then carried out surveys on a variety of other countries and found, to his surprise, that a similar distribution applied.

A chart that gave the effect a very visible and comprehensible form, the so-called "champagne glass" effect, was contained in the 1992 United Nations Development Program Report, which showed that distribution of global income is very uneven, with the richest 20% of the world's population receiving 82.7% of the world's income. However, among nations, the Gini index shows that wealth distributions vary substantially around this norm.

Distribution of world GDP, 1989[11]

Quintile of population	Income
Richest 20%	82.70%
Second 20%	11.75%
Third 20%	2.30%
Fourth 20%	1.85%
Poorest 20%	1.40%

The principle also holds within the tails of the distribution. The physicist Victor Yakovenko of the University of Maryland, College Park, and AC Silva analyzed income data from the US Internal Revenue Service from 1983 to 2001 and found that the income distribution of the richest 1–3% of the population also follows Pareto's principle.

So how does MLM and the Pareto Principle stand up against a "prestigious" career in real estate? I stumbled across this blog online from:

https://www.relitix.com/blog/how-rare-are-high-producing-agents   I decided to include it in its entirety. I could not have said it better myself

Let's take a look at what one real estate agent found (MLS Data):

Does the 80/20 rule really apply to real estate agents?

The *80/20 rule*, more properly known as the *Pareto principle*, states that, for many events, 80% of the effects come from 20% of the causes. First developed as a means of describing land ownership in Italy in the 1800s, the rule has since been adopted by economists, management gurus, sports medicine, and a myriad of other fields.

"Since my earliest days in real estate I've heard this rule applied to agents: 80% of the production comes from 20% of the agents. While it always "felt" correct, I never bothered to actually check the facts. Well . . . now we can.

Looking at 120,000 real estate agents in rural and urban markets throughout the country, we find that it's not quite as unbalanced as 80/20.

The actual ratio for real estate agents is almost exactly 75/25.

That is to say that 75% of the production is done by the top 25% of agents or teams. This ratio is nearly identical if we consider closed sides instead of dollars (detailed results below). If you are curious about that 80% number, it turns out that **the top 30% of the agents produce 80% of the results.** This production, while skewed, is not quite as unequal as most of us thought.

Notes:

Percentage of agents closing 80% of volume: 29.02%

Percentage of agents closing 80% of sides: 30.27%

Percentage of agents closing 75.33% of volume: 24.66%

Percentage of agents closing 74.75% of sides: 25.25%

Production measured May 2018–April 2019 on 120,000 real estate agents who had at least one closing during the period May 2017– April 2019.

Agents are defined as individual MLS entities and may include teams aggregating under a single name.

How rare are high-producing agents?[11]

We all know top-producing agents. We see their ads everywhere. Their signs are in yards throughout the market. But how many of them are there? How narrow is that pyramid?

It turns out that it is very narrow, indeed. Looking at one hundred thousand-plus agents from markets around the country who had at least one closing during the prior year, let's group them by their total twelve- month closings—for example, we'll have a group which closed $1M–$2M during that time frame. When we plot the number of agents in each group, we get a chart that looks like this:

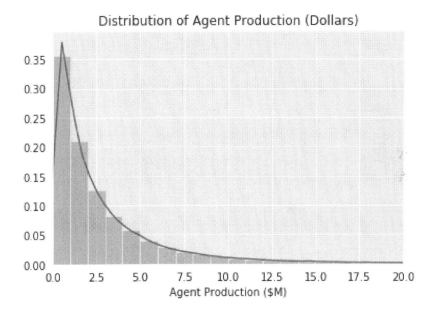

11   https://www.relitix.com/blog/how-rare-are-high-producing-agents

This graph (officially known as a *histogram*) shows that the number of agents at higher production levels declines at an exponential rate. In fact, if we remove the nearly 20% of agents who posted zero production during the year, the graph describes a nearly perfect exponential curve.

What does this mean for the rarity of high producers? Imagine that we took one hundred agents who had at least one closing during the twelve months from May 2017-April 2018 and put them all on two Greyhound buses, making them board in order of how many dollars they closed during May 2018 - April 2019.

The front half of the first bus would be filled by agents without a single closing. The rest of that first bus would be filled by agents who closed less than $1M. Halfway through filling the second bus we would still only be at $3M. Each of the last 4 agents in line, the last row, would have closed more than $10M with the very last agent posting $27M.

The figure of 48% of agents doing less than $1M per year in closings is especially stark when you remember that we are only considering agents who had some production in the prior twelve months. If we were to look at all licensees, the proportion who produce less than $1M would likely rise to nearly 2/3. Unproductive agents are more than common—they are the norm.

Agents who produce more than $10M per year in closings comprised less than 6% of the total pool of agents who had a closing the last two years. $20M agents are around 1.5% of that pool. Rare indeed!

So where is the uproar? Where are the critics? Where are the Facebook and Reddit groups dedicated to exposing this scam? Why don't your family and friends tell all the horror stories of people they know that "failed" in real estate? Where are the lawsuits and the government watch groups and the three-letter agencies investigating these companies that recruit these poor, helpless, unsuspecting victims of these big meanie real estate companies? Why are the victims not complaining about their lost investment in time, money, and resources! Why are we not up in arms about the fact that "only the people at the top make money!" WTF!

CHAPTER 7

START A TRADITIONAL BUSINESS, THEY SAID

If you take this a step further and look at business failures in general. You really start to scratch your head.

Business failure rate across industries[12]

Industry	Business failure rate within 1 year	Business failure rate after 5 years	Business failure rate after 10 years
Mining, quarrying and oil and gas extraction	25.6%	58.5%	74.8%

---

12   https://www.lendingtree.com/business/small/failure-rate/.

Administrative and waste services	20.9%	49.1%	66.9%
Information	20.8%	51.7%	73.3%
Arts, entertainment and recreation	18.9%	42.6%	66.5%
Wholesale trade	17.5%	47.5%	70.5%
Construction	17.1%	41.4%	62.4%
Professional, scientific and technical services	17.1%	47.7%	70.3%
Educational services	17.0%	40.8%	63.6%
Utilities	16.2%	40.4%	55.6%
Transportation and warehousing	16.2%	47.0%	67.3%
Management of companies and enterprises	16.2%	48.6%	63.0%

Finance and insurance	15.3%	43.3%	63.2%
Other services (except public administration)	15.1%	40.7%	61.7%
Accommodation and food services	14.7%	40.4%	64.3%
Manufacturing	14.4%	38.7%	58.8%
Health care and social assistance	14.1%	44.1%	60.8%
Retail trade	12.4%	38.1%	60.6%
Agriculture, forestry, fishing and hunting	12.3%	30.0%	48.1%
Real estate and rental and leasing	11.6%	35.1%	59.8%

Here's the full list of the top reasons startups fail, from CB Insights:[13]

13   https://www.lendingtree.com/business/small/failure-rate/

- Ran out of money/couldn't raise new capital: 38%

- Lack of market need: 35%

- Beat by competition: 20%

- Wrong business model: 19%

- Regulatory/legal hurdles: 18%

- Didn't properly price things: 15%

- Wrong team members: 14%

- Bad timing for product: 10%

- Flawed product: 8%

- Friction among team/investors: 7%

- Failed pivot: 6%

- Burned out/no passion: 5%

The majority of business owners will not make it past 10 years regardless of the industry.

Here is the rub:

How many traditional business owners do you think went all in and invested more than $1,000? Quit their full-time jobs? Borrowed money, mortgaged the house, put in long hours, and still couldn't make it work long-term? The numbers are staggering.

How much does it cost to run a business?

According to our research, small-business owners spend an average of $40,000 in their first full year of business. We also asked our respondents to take it one step further—we had them look back at their first-year records and tell us how much money they allocated to various business expenses as a percentage of their total budget. To keep it simple, we bucketed the following functions and cost categories:

- Product: raw materials, inventory, supplier, manufacturing, patents, etc.

- Operating: incorporation/legal fees, accounting software and services, etc.

- Online store: website/platform subscription, hosting and domain name, contract developer/designer, etc.

- Shipping: packaging, labels, etc.

- Offline: stall/table fees, office space, rent, gas, etc.

- Team/staff: salaries, benefits, perks, etc.

- Marketing: logo, branding, ads, printed materials, etc.

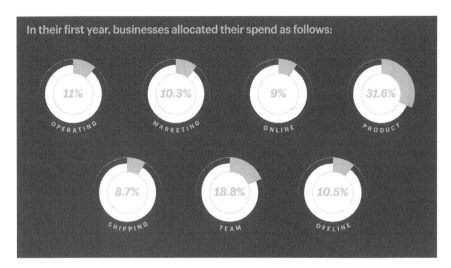

In their first year, small businesses spent:

- 11% on operating costs

- 10.3% on marketing costs

- 9% on online costs

- 31.6% on product costs

- 8.7% on shipping costs

- 18.8% on team costs

- 10.5% on offline costs

It's important to note that the amount businesses spent in their first year varied significantly, depending on factors like industry and business model; whether the business was a full-time, part-time, or hobby venture; and whether the business had additional employees.

Sources of financing for early-stage founders

While new entrepreneurs often rely on their personal savings to keep their business afloat in the early days, one-third of respondents reported reinvesting revenue from their business sales to cover their business costs in the first year.

Top funding sources for business owners:*

- Personal savings (66%)

- Reinvesting sales revenue (30%)

- Financial support from friends and family (23%)

- Personal loan (21%)

* Respondents could select more than one funding source[14]

So when we look at an example of a startup network marketing company (less than two years new) like O'Snap Active Lifestyle with approximately four thousand total brand ambassadors, how many do you think are actually active? Probably 5%–20% max!

The majority of brand ambassadors invested less than $150, and a small percentage went "all in" and invested a whopping $1,000. The active requirement in the O'snap Active Lifestyle is one customer per month, or you can fulfill the active requirement with a personal purchase of one product. (approximately $60 with an immediate payout of $15 on a retail customer and additional commissions accumulating in other areas of the compensation plan). How many do you think even show

14   Roxanne Voidonicolas, "Starting Up," Nov. 8, 2022. Shopify.com.

up for the first training? How many do you think actually jump on an hour-short corporate communication Zoom? How many do you think registered themselves on the automation app? Less than 10%! As my mentor Jim Rohn would to say, "Not a good number."

If we were playing any sport and only 10% even bothered to show up for practice, how do you think we would perform in the actual game? Exactly! Would the fans blame the sport? Or blame the coach and the players? MLM is the only sport that not only do the fans blame the sport, but the players that never showed up and the coaches that never coached also blame the sport! It's insane!

Here is how you know it's a bunch of crock: The vast majority will blame the company, the products, and the compensation plan—basically everything except themselves—and then go join another company! Then they will proceed to do the exact same thing again. Deep down they know it's them and not the opportunity.

How do I know?

Well, sadly, I was one of them.

CHAPTER 8

I'VE MET THE ENEMY,
AND HE IS ME

We met the players that showed up. We witnessed the lifestyles of the real hard-working, dedicated coaches. We know we didn't do what we were supposed to do. We know we didn't follow the system. We know we took shortcuts. We know we are liars! But why take responsibility?

We'd rather be like this: "I called three of my friends! I'm kinda entitled to success. It's my birthright! Might as well blame the big, bad company that provided me with an opportunity to learn while I earn, to be mentored by leaders who actually made it happen, who invested the resources for me to have a shot at the entrepreneurial dream. Besides, my friend just called me about this 'new and improved' company! They have the best product, that Elon Musk himself said they will take to Mars! Pretty sure it cures every major disease known to man. The compensation plan pays out 235% on zero volume! People are going intergalactic crown black diamond in the first week. The owners are Mark Cuban's, Warren Buffet's, and Richard Branson's bro-n-laws.

They are the best, highest educated, richest entrepreneurs that ever lived that you've never heard of. They feed starving children, shelter the homeless and go to church every day! All the Sharks on *Shark Tank* wanted this product, but no way! This is our super-exclusive quadruple-patented proprietary secret! If you get in right now, we will virtually put every leader under you! You will just cash checks every minute! Everyone makes money just posting selfies on Instagram!"

Who wouldn't join that? Well, anyone with some damn business sense.

What do you think is going to happen? I'll tell you, a ton will join, and most will drop off their hard-earned money and wait to get rich. Can you blame them? They were never taught in school how to identify a real opportunity. Even if the company is totally legit. They have been set up to fail from the first hyped-up word spit out of their new sponsor's mouth! The greed from the upline allows this nonsense: "Well, what if she is the one? We can't tell the truth, or she may not join! Lies are easy. Tell them exactly what they want to hear. Tell them no work, big fortunes. Just get 'em in!" And the cycle continues. I've seen self-proclaimed "leaders" jump from three-plus MLMs in a single year, never once blaming themselves.

They make all the money on the upfront hype. When that runs dry, which it inevitably will, they move on.

At least if they would admit they are looking to get rich quick without actually doing the work, or that they are just horrific at choosing and evaluating business opportunities, or that they have never seen anything through to the end in their entire life, or my personal favorite, that God didn't actually tell them to go to the last three companies, that was just indigestion, at least we could follow them for their honesty.

In the long run, they actually hurt the very profession they are attempting to extract gold from. Think about it. They know they are going to leave the company. Why wouldn't they? They already did as much as their skill set would allow. They have duplicated what they have seen other "leaders" do. They are clueless on how to actually scale a business, how to actually develop leaders. They have zero interest in grinding it out for years like real business owners do.

They know how to create drama. Hype people up and sell the possibility of massive fortune by being in early with them.

The game plan is super obvious. I've seen it hundreds of times. They first plant seeds of doubt with anyone who will listen in the current organization. This is easy to do. Remember, most made a small investment believing they were going to get massive returns. Most made a call or two, posted corny spammy stuff on their Facebook page, and did not generate much interest. Now all you have to do is tell them it's not their fault: "Of course it's the company, the product, the leadership. You should be making millions by now. After all, you're a rock star! You have been in for nine whole months! But don't worry, I have something up my sleeve for us!! What a joke! Within a few weeks they will post their public service announcement that they have found the new holy grail of opportunities and will lead everyone to the promised land! The cycle continues.

CHAPTER 9

2 WAYS TO HAVE THE TALLEST BUILDING, BUILD IT, OR TEAR DOWN EVERYONE ELSE'S

We, the very distributors, continue to tarnish the entire profession by overpromising, underdelivering, putting down other distributors, and talking smack about other companies. Just today at the gym, one of our reps told me someone from another company was trying to recruit her. She told this person she was happy and not interested in another opportunity. A professional that thinks long-term and cares about the integrity of the entire profession should have said something like, "Congratulations on finding a home in our incredible industry. I wish you nothing but massive success. Please let me know if I can assist or if anything changes in the future." Here is what this jackball did instead: lied! told this brand-new, fragile person, who is also new to the entire industry, that she should "be careful." This goof said he knew me, and to make it sound more believable, he added details. He said he went to school with me! WTF! Those that know me know I didn't go to school! Lol! he went on to say my company isn't doing well and heard it was being sold! Ugh!

Sooner or later this lie would be exposed, but the damage had already been done, and another person will blame the profession instead of this clown (I have another name for him, but will refrain as to keep this book PG AF), making the entire profession look like crap!

Update: This distributor ended up joining the other company. The truth was definitely not as palatable as the lie. What starts on a lie will inevitably die on a lie. The negative cycle continues.

CHAPTER 10

COMPANIES SUCK TOO!

The other side to this coin is the companies that purposefully prey on these people. They make shoddy overpriced products. They put a ton of "gotchas" in the compensation plan. They "prop" up certain leaders. And most provide little to no training, systems, or tools for their distributors. It's the "go get 'em tiger" mentality. They are laundering money amongst friends. "Wink ,wink don't tell anyone the product is just an excuse to drive a compensation plan for the handful of chosen ones that are in on the deal. It's a game only a few that started it or are in on it know how to play. It's rigged." By the way, there are usually lots of clues that this is happening. The owners have done this before. Check their history. What are other people that were in business with them saying? Do they leave a wake of debt and disappointment everywhere they go? Past indictments are also a pretty big red flag for me.

Some companies allow greed to drive the entire operation. It's a cash grab for sure. Have you heard the phrase "buyer beware"? We should be closely evaluating all business opportunities. It's our own fault if we do zero due diligence. We deserve what we get.

Choose your company wisely. Not all companies are created equal. Not all have your best interest in mind. In fact, I'll go out on a limb and say most don't. Evaluate the company like you would evaluate your brain surgeon, your child's college, or your future spouse—or at least as much as you would your next two-week vacation destination.

Evaluate these six areas:

1. **People:** track record, integrity

2. **Product:** viable, unique, non me too, consumable, relevant

3. **Process:** simple, efficient, effective, automated

4. **Community:** supportive, humble, competent

5. **Culture:** service, happy, winning, purposeful

6. **Compensation:** competitive, fair, rewarding, potentially very lucrative

I listed them in the order of importance. A lot of network marketers would argue with me about this. I get hit all the time with the "my compensation plan is better than yours" nonsense. Yeah, and you're selling air or some BS product that no one would actually purchase if you didn't have that compensation plan attached to it. That's not a good business model to stake your future on.

Network marketing is the lowest risk, lowest overhead way for the average, ordinary person to start a business. Just because it's low risk in comparison to every other type of business, make sure you understand what it takes to succeed. The two main factors are pipeline (how many people you're asking if they are open) and perspective (where you spend the majority of your time in your mind). Thinking negatively and hardly talking to anyone are the main reasons for failing.

— Ray Higdon

CHAPTER 11

LOTTERY MENTALITY

So why do we keep coming back? It's simple, and it's right there in the dreaded income disclosure statements! Some pretty ordinary people actually do get very rich doing this. Where else can you turn a $1,000 initial investment into millions of dollars? That, my friend, is both the blessing and the curse of this profession.

The blessing is obvious. You can make some damn good money if you get this right. You can also have what most employees and small business owners never seem to have enough of: time freedom. You also don't have the student loans, income caps, racial inequality, background checks, glass ceilings, and crappy bosses found in most employment scenarios.

The curse is also obvious. People treat it like a lottery ticket. By the way, I have never seen lottery payouts this large in my history. More people than ever are willing to buy lottery tickets (weekly) for not much less than an MLM startup fee—with massive odds that the money is gone forever! You can easily point to people all over the profession who are making lottery-type money: Terry Lacore, Jason Caramanis, Josh and

Jenna Zwagil, Jessie Lee Ward, Stormy Wellington, Darnell Self, Brian Caruthers, Josh Denne, Holton Buggs, Larry Smith, Mike Humes, Jeff Olson, Tim Her, Ray Higdon, Dan Stammen, Eddie Parker, Matt Morris, Jefferson Santos, Anthony Napolitano, Alex Morton, Danny Kirby, Ron Williams, Kim Melia, Mike Fedick, Jermaine Johnson, Frazer Brookes, Jesse Macpherson, Mayor Chris Brown, Alfred Nichson, Eric Worre, Patrick Shaw, Tony and Sarah Zolecki, Rabu Gary, Kelly Vincent, Tina Malsom, John and Nadya Melton, Jason Nemes, Sarah Fontenot, Lissette Pettis, Michelle Game, Lisa Grossman, Kurtis Broom, Daryl Drake, Darin Kid, Jeremy Roma, and Najlah Malott are just a few of my millionaire MLM friends that put in the work.

So why not buy the ticket, or in this case put up your small initial investment? The only reason this doesn't work is because people didn't work. When they inevitably officially quit, they tell everyone it's a scam, but they forget to disclose the most important fact: They didn't do jack shit! They couldn't sell their family and friends on the product or opportunity, but they sure sold them on the idea of it being a scam! People will say, "You poor thing! Just another victim of these horrible pyramid schemes."

OK, so we have seen the good, the bad, and the ugly. Now what? What the hell am I supposed to do?

> "One of the best things about our industry is that you can get paid your worth. Conversely, one of the scariest things about our industry

is that you get paid your worth. The good news is... everyone has the ability to grow regardless of their starting point. The bad news is... you can't fake growth. I'm so grateful that I'm not the same person who started my Network Marketing career over 2 decades ago and I'm even more grateful that our teams' incomes are a direct reflection of that."

- **Darnell Self**

CHAPTER 12

YOU CAN MAKE EXCUSES OR YOU CAN MAKE MONEY, BUT YOU CAN'T MAKE BOTH

In my opinion, the #1 reason so many people fail to build real financial abundance and freedom is because of the way they're being taught. Think about it this way: if you have a great product, which is probably a big reason you were drawn in initially, and you've got a financial model that creates an opportunity for earnings, others are clearly winning. Then why isn't it working?

Is it that you're not getting in front of enough people? Or maybe you don't know enough about sales? You don't know anybody? You're an introvert? You don't have a big social media following? You're too young? You're too old? You live in a small town? You live in a big city? Maybe this just isn't for you? I've heard it all.

The real reason? Besides the fact that you don't understand the game you are in, you don't have the real coaching, tools, or support you need. Now, sure, your upline probably sent you a few scripts or had you list out one hundred-plus friends, family members, and random acquaintances in an attempt to have you begin hitting the phones. But most likely, your upline is just as clueless as you. After all, they are just duplicating the same bad behavior they were exposed to. They are praying you are the winning lottery ticket.

Maybe your company has a few videos and training sessions that have given you the toolkit to begin working on growing a team and distributing products. They keep telling you to "follow the system," but WTF is the system! They don't seem to have clear answers.

Network marketing, when done right, is one of the most lucrative earning opportunities, allowing you to build an empire and legacy that can be passed down for generations. Think Dexter Yager.

This means it should be treated as a tool and as a real business (I'll touch on this later) rather than a side hustle or extra hobby, in which you sporadically spam your friends with texts and Facebook messages. That's not to say that you have to spend endless hours working your business each week! You just need to understand the approach, use your time well, and find ways to systemize and automate your process.

My reputation as the Anti-MLM Network Marketer came about because, frankly, I'm tired of seeing greedy uplines, coaches, gurus, and top reps in many of these companies teaching you all of the old recruiting and sales techniques from ten or twenty years ago or, even worse, the new-school grab-and-jump mentality. Do these techniques still work? Sometimes. But those are not the real ways you're going to build a lasting business that allows you to scale, automate, and enjoy the financial and time freedom you're after!

A lot of the time they really don't know what to do. The rules change weekly. What they did five years ago can't possibly work today. The old-school philosophy of throw enough at the wall and some of it will stick is a terrible strategy today.

Another challenge is weak leaders build weak leaders. They are praying that you are the strong one! They hope that you are the one, in spite of your lack of skills, all the obstacles, the naysayers, and your lack of information, that somehow will go to the top. Of course this happens, but it is certainly the exception, not the rule.

All too often it's the blind leading the blind in a big-ass circle. Everyone is waiting for the next person to make them rich! Guess what happens? No one gets rich!

Inevitably your upline will leave. BTW, I hate the words *upline, downline,* etc. Look, no one wants to be downline, downwind, or whatever. I'll give you better names later.

Anyway, they will leave, but, worse, they will make a major announcement on social media. They will complain about the company, the leaders, the product, and whatever excuses they can drum up. Here is what they will not do: say they were idiots, that they were not equipped and they didn't take initiative to learn or put in the work. They may say they are done, retiring, taking a break, or whatever. But this is all a setup! MLM is in the bloodstream. It's their "lottery ticket." And it's difficult to let it go for long. Sooner or later the announcement will come: "GOD has shown me my new opportunity." This one is different because of the things we've already discussed—basically the same BS they said about the last opportunity.

Listen, I believe in GOD. What I don't believe is he keeps leading you in and out of network marketing companies every eight months!

Either GOD is wrong or you're reading the tea leaves wrong. Either way I wouldn't follow!

Let me arm you with a few of my favorite modern-day methods that will help you bring in new customers and distributors consistently each and every month without feeling like you have to mass message your friends or family members with a ten-page script or corny word plays on the phone.

STEP #1: Change your mindset, change your approach.

For many people, building a home-based business may be your first or second step into the world of entrepreneurship and, really, running your own organization. With anything, mental toughness is one of the most important prerequisites to success in any business, job, or task you're working toward.

Why?

Because the inevitable tough times will always come about. I can say with complete confidence that at some point in your journey, you will be tested. Whether it's in your personal life or business, there will come a time that you'll have to rely on your mental toughness and strategic persistence to get you through.

I can't count how many times I quit while building. Man, this stuff can be too much at times! The key was I never quit out loud or publicly. I took the rest of the day to sulk, complain to my support person, lie in bed, cry, or whatever, and then I was back at it the next day.

After a while I developed rhino skin. It became fun dealing with the bad apples, the negative Nancys. I just had to get a little better than the majority of mediocre people who were trying to slow me down. My wanting to win became stronger than their ignorant objections.

Mastering your mindset is not the hard part. In fact, I believe it is simply a series of mental shifts. The hard part is consistency and accountability when it comes time to exercise your "mental muscle," so let's start with the basics.

Shift #1 Believe in yourself and what you're doing. You have to be resilient and able to continue building what you believe is the next best thing. Not everyone will believe in what you're doing. In fact, if you haven't experienced it already . . . you may be surprised at the people who doubt you or go against your vision.

Shift #2 Think three steps ahead. I follow my gut, and I play chess, not checkers. Think of every opportunity three steps ahead in every possible direction. Even if it seems like something would benefit me immediately, it might not benefit me in the long run. Don't just ask yourself, "What is happening right now?" but, "What will happen three steps from the action I'm going to take today?" This is how you become a leader worthy of a large organization. This is how you become a person of respect.

Shift #3 Do the hardest thing first. The hardest thing is usually the thing you should be going after. Chances are nobody else is, or at least very few people are. It is essential that you get used to the uncomfortable feeling of not being the best—*yet*—and learn how to channel that as the fuel to wake up every day and strive to be better.

Shift *#4* Think big and small. You have to learn to think big and small. You have to go in the same direction with small day-to-day decisions, as well as big actions.

Once you are on your way, you will mostly have to occupy yourself with little things, which can be tedious. I call it "mastering the mundane." At times, you're going to have to buck up and do the work that has to be done (the small things), even if you're not great at it or don't enjoy it. After all, getting a lot of people doing a little bit is what truly scales well. (Think Mcdonald's.)

It is so important to be able to step back, look at the big picture, and give direction to the overall vision, whether it's leading yourself or leading your team.

Shift *#5* Create your own luck. So-called lucky people aren't necessarily getting more advantages than other people. The universe doesn't favor them—the harsh reality is that they are probably working harder and/or smarter than you are. They're putting themselves out there more. They're creating more connections that could lead to other stuff. If you have big goals, you're going to have to put in a big effort, not just wait for your lucky break. My experience has been the harder I worked, the "luckier" I became.

Shift *#6* Give. Give. Give. For me, I've had twenty-nine years in the profession. That's like a thousand dog years! I've gone from struggling distributor to multi-million-dollar earner to owner of my own network marketing company. I have learned all of the right, wrong, best, and worst ways to do nearly everything in this profession. What good does it do for me to keep all of that bottled up in my own head?

I just don't save my best tips for myself. Instead, I try to share them, on social media, in resources like this, on stages, on Zooms, and in my daily interactions! Helping and sharing is content marketing, which is one of the best ways to build a business nowadays! It also makes our profession, well, more professional.

Build an audience, and determine what they need and want from you. Create content, attract your audience, and build your business. Whether you have years in this profession or not, you have value to add. Maybe you're skilled in social media, leadership, technology, or sales. Find a skill, or learn one that you can share with others.

Take this seriously. Focus on a skill you have or develop one that makes you stand out. Do not skip this, and do not take it for granted.

You must stand out in a crowded, competitive environment.

Step #2: Leverage digital marketing.

Facebook Messenger and Text Messages: I've surprised myself quite a bit with this one, but today, this is one of my favorite network marketing tools. I used to stay away from Facebook Messenger thinking it was the biggest thief of time and the best way to get distracted in my business. But I have to say, **there's a right and a wrong way to use Facebook Messenger, and I've figured out how to use it the right way**.

Using messages, regardless of *how* you send them, should be about creating new relationships, inciting curiosity, and driving traffic to your opportunity.

Now you may be thinking, "What's new about this? I've been told to text people before."

Well, the difference here is simple.

I want you to spend more time focusing specifically on the following:

1. **Who you'd like to connect with** - Who is your target audience, what type of people do you want to join you? What do they like to do for fun? How old are they? What do they currently do for work?

2. **What motivates these people?** - Are they craving financial freedom? Are they looking to sharpen a specific skill? Are they wanting more fulfillment or a sense of belonging?

3. **How do you relate to them?** Were you in this situation yourself? Did you see someone close to you experience this? Have you helped others achieve it?

For years I've heard even the *top* coaches in this industry telling people to send out the same run-of-the-mill messages. Chances are your uplines may have taught you to do this as well. The difference is customization and connection. The best way to drive traffic is by getting clear on the specific type of people you are talking to!

Traditional business owners know their target market, and you should too. I know you were told it's a numbers game. That's true, but it should be targeted to people you relate to and relate back to you. The more narrow that focus in the beginning, the better.

If you understand the type of person that your product or opportunity can benefit, you're going to have so much more success in really communicating with them. So take the time to outline who you want to talk to. What type of person would benefit from having the opportunity to work with you? Maybe someone who lost their job due to a pandemic? Maybe someone who hasn't been able to take time off of work for the past five years and feels like they are missing out on the best years of their kids growing up? Maybe it's someone who is a really skilled sales and marketing professional in the corporate world who isn't getting paid what their talents are worth! Maybe it's a school teacher who wants to help people but is not feeling fulfilled.

In those simple examples, you've got different pain points, completely different points of motivation, all different perspectives on how something like this could help them. So do you think a, "Hey, bud, I know we haven't talked since high school, but I think that you could totally kill it with a new side hustle," text is going to work universally? Of course not! Put yourself in their shoes and think about what really, truly motivates them. Then find the best way to spark that conversation and properly position your message.

In my experience, less is always more.

So what makes our Facebook Messenger approach different from simply sending a text or email?

Facebook is creating more and more opportunities for automation by leveraging a tool called chatbots. These can be set up directly through the platform or using third party tools like Many Chat and ChatGPT. I do predict artificial intelligence is going to dramatically change and streamline the way we communicate. Embrace it or get left in the dust.

A chatbot can simulate the conversation based on someone's response, just like those "pick your path" books that you may remember from school! If they say yes, they will get a different response than if they say no.

I won't get into all of the possible paths that you can go down with this, as everyone's offer is going to be different depending on the company you are with or the product you offer. But I want you to take the first step in having these conversations manually and really defining your specific audiences in order to make it easier to set up down the road!

ChatGPT/Artificial intelligence: This requires an entire book itself. Learn it! The possibilities are endless. This alone will dramatically improve your efficiency and results. This may be the single biggest breakthrough for network marketers ever.

Webinars: Webinars are a great way to leverage the way for you to do your network marketing presentations! But again, this shouldn't just be the same old, same old everything you've been told to do. It's important to again focus on who you are trying to communicate with and what they need to hear.

Webinars and online training allow you to have a bigger impact on more people and build a tool that in the future you can automate and scale.

Create a webinar where you talk about the benefits of network marketing, why your company is good, how it has helped you, and why (specifically) it can help someone in (x) situation.

Once you have a presentation ready to go, practice it a few times and try recording yourself! This tool will go a long way in your business because you can distribute it in many different forms! For example, in your messages, text, or Facebook, when you're sending them to view it, they actually see *you* and hear your voice and your story, which makes it much more personable and easier for your prospect to connect with.

You've probably heard this before, but the fastest way to drive a sale is by building *know, like,* and *trust.* You want people to like you, like what you have to offer; know you and feel like they are getting to connect with a real person, not just another salesperson with a bad case of commission breath; and trust that you're genuinely interested in helping them find success and results with both your product and your opportunity! The tools we have today driven by social media, Messenger, Zoom, and many others allow us to speed up the whole *know, like,* and *trust* thing.

Step #3: Lead with value – What else can you provide that's valuable? Personal development with a paycheck.

In general, you should always go into any interaction with the intention of adding value, particularly when growing a network marketing business.

Ask yourself what else you can do to not only attract new prospects with value, but to also support your existing downline with tools and resources that will help them thrive in their efforts as well. The more people that you can help, the more momentum you build, causing a snowball effect of lives impacted and changed forever, and to me . . . that is what building a legacy is all about.

Keep *value* top of mind as you tackle your business-building tasks each day.

Be willing to sacrifice the short-term buck for long-term wealth.

STEP #4: Community effort . . . often called *duplication* or *scaling*.

Find a way to get your team working together. Humans are inherently social; we crave community and belonging. This is natural and can be healthy. That need for belonging can go haywire, however, when it morphs into pack mentality.

Pack mentality (also known as *herd mentality*, *mob mentality*, or *gang mentality*), unlike community building, is defined by elements of hostility and fear: If you're within the pack, you better play by the rules or risk getting kicked out.

This can happen in two different ways: through physical community and your leadership.

But the reality is, people love to feel like they are a part of something, something bigger than themselves. That is a huge part of network marketing, selling the vision and the culture and supporting your community to bring their visions to life!

In terms of creating a physical community, to encourage duplication, a few of the methods I recommend implementing sooner than later are things like the following:

1. Creating a team Facebook group, where you collaborate, provide support, highlight successes, give tips and insights, and even run different contests or incentives! A lot of people that join network marketing companies are craving a level of connection that they otherwise aren't getting! Maybe they didn't have many close friendships and wanted to be a part of something! After all, connection is a core human desire that everyone craves to some degree. Play into that sense of belonging by creating a community! This may even become a recruiting tool and something that they use as a unique value offer to new prospects that they are looking to invite!

2. Reward benchmarks outside of the company structure, create different incentives that encourage your team to stay active, and continue to self-motivate. The reality is, the more your organization grows, the more you're going to have to.

3. Nothing fancy. In the movie *Hitch*, Will Smith's character Alex, "Hitch," is hired to teach Kevin James' character, Albert, how

to get a girl way out of his league. Part of that is to teach Albert to dance without embarrassing himself. Albert wants to go crazy when the music comes on! Pop locking, the running man, the sprinkler, and the cue tip are his go-to moves. It's actually hilarious! In the movie, Hitch slaps Albert across the face (funny how real life sometimes imitates art) and tells him to never, ever do that kind of dancing again! He proceeds to show him a simple two-step back and forth, keeping it simple and cool, saying, "This is where you live." Creating a large organization is like this. You can't have fancy footwork. It cannot be complex, confusing, or even too corny. Your team has to be able to duplicate what you do. They have to want to duplicate what you do. If not, you're going to just spin in circles.

4. Have a few steps for everything. I subscribe to the rule of three. I have three steps for prospecting, three steps for exposing, three steps for closing, and three steps for onboarding. I'm systematic in everything I do. In fact, most of it is now video based and automated.

5. Play together! Have fun together, and schedule activities. We've rented roller rinks, bowling alleys, limousines, tickets to sporting events, days at the park or beach, cruise ships, hotels, etc. Don't be all business all the time!

Step #5: Create content/be active on social media.

Love it or hate it, it's here to stay. Billions of people scrolling mindlessly on these platforms makes for some interesting opportunities. Embrace it, study it, and use it as a tool to build your business. These opportunities certainly didn't exist when I was coming up.

Contrary to most beliefs, a bigger following does not make for a more successful business. Posting trending reels on Instagram is a great way to expose people to you, your company, and your product. But it's not *the* marketing strategy; it's simply part of it. The notion that we can post some cool content on TikTok and we will be set for life is mind-boggling and unrealistic.

Millions of people posting content are not making a dime. However, I've done very well on social media. I studied it, I hired mentors, and I put myself out there. Like most things, trial and error were my best teachers. Being successful with social media requires consistency and commitment. I have another book coming soon on my exact social media strategy.

How social media has ruined you!

Back in the day, we had what we called the three-foot rule. If you came within three feet of someone, you had to pitch to them. It was hands-on, immediate feedback. If you sucked, you knew it. The prospect let you know it and your results showed it. If you want to win, you better get good really fast. We worked on our communication, our approach, and our close. We attended actual live training to get better. We even paid money to attend! We showed up to live presentations every week to learn the actual pitch—rain, sleet, or snow! We didn't accept excuses. We had leaders with heart and courage, and we were creating millionaires! This was serious business. We knew what it took, and we did it, at first on faith.

My friend **Stormy Wellington** says, "The challenge today is most want to be Facebook and Instagram gangsters." But relying on a few posts on social media or even a lot of posts does not make your business. It sounds great when the gurus tell you to stay home, make reels on Instagram, and get rich. But this is usually followed by, "Buy my coaching package." The fact is, you will need to connect with people. I'm sorry, but if you could just sit around and post on social media, the company wouldn't need you.

Step #6 Show up and show out.

Attend everything. Yes, everything! The question is, how bad do you want it? Schedule the next Zoom, live event, opportunity presentation, and training right now. Make it a priority. Everyone is watching. When your friends call you to go bowling on Tuesday but there is training on Tuesday, let them know loud and proud: "I have a business event, sorry!" This is not a game to you. You are different. You are going to the top because you are willing to do what most won't. You will one day have what most won't as well. That's the type of person worthy of following. When you show up, contribute, own the room, and act as if you are already at the top position.

Step #7 Sponsor up.

Find people smarter, faster, more successful than you. This may be one of my best tactics. I once had a mentor say " I'd rather be rejected by a millionaire than a homeless person" I understood what he was saying. We are going to get rejection. There is no way around that fact. So why not go after the best and the brightest. Its your business. Think in terms of who would you hire to work for you, The best most qualified or the bottom of the barrel. People will always get this twisted. They will say "So you want me to prejudge people?" YES! Not in the way that society judges. Judge based on these 3 characteristics and I believe you will be fine.

1. Burning Desire

2. Willing to work

3. Coachable / Teachable / Humble

CHAPTER 13

WORK LIKE YOU'RE AFRAID TO BE FIRED (EVEN IF YOU'RE NOT)

> **YES, IT IS TRUE, MOST FAIL IN NETWORK MARKETING, AND YOU PROBABLY WILL, TOO, IF YOU DON'T UNDERSTAND THE GAME YOU ARE IN AND THE RULES TO PLAY THE GAME!**

One of the most popular pieces of bullshit advice given in MLM is this: "Treat your business like a hobby and you'll get paid like a hobby. Treat your business like a business and you'll get paid like a business." Have you heard this? It's what I heard early in my career, and it sounded good, so I started sharing the same message with my team. But wait . . . having your own "business" gives you complete freedom. You have the freedom to work whenever you want and the freedom to work however much you want. Doesn't it? So for over 90 percent of networkers, this means you work an hour or two a week or less. If something comes up, like a new movie you want to see, you go see the movie because your "business" gives you the freedom to do so. This "freedom" is part of why over 90 percent fail.

Let me be direct with you: I didn't become a full-time leader in network marketing because I treated my MLM business like a business with this kind of freedom. I made it because I treated my business like a dirty little word in our profession: A JOB! (~gasp~) That's right—I treated my business like a job! You see, in a job, if you only show up some of the time, what happens? If you decide to go to the movie instead of showing up for work, what happens? If you sleep in when you were supposed to be at work, what happens? Exactly: you get fired! The reason most fail in MLM is because they can't get fired. If you have a job and you know you'll get fired if you don't show up, you show up! If you have a job and you know you'll get fired if you don't do the work, you do the work! Somehow, though, networkers have this "dream" that they can achieve unlimited freedom, riches, and recognition by acting as if they have the freedom to do whatever they want. I'm going to let you in on a secret: It just ain't so! I made it and all the leaders I've worked with who made it did so because we showed up and treated our business like a job! When we didn't feel like coming in to work, we showed up. When we were tired, we showed up. When we didn't feel like doing the work, we did the work. So don't fall victim to this whole concept of being able to treat your business like a business. Treat your business like a job. Because freedom ain't free—you gotta work for it! Period, point blank!

Show up every day! Consistency is the real game changer. How hard is it to win when the other team shows up sometimes, if at all?

Make your business a priority. If your company or team leadership has a weekly Zoom, never miss it. NEVER! My mentor Jim Rohn used to say, "You don't ask a farmer to go bowling during harvest time." It should be crystal clear to everyone that certain days and times are just completely off--limits. They would not expect you to help them move or go to the baseball game during your scheduled work hours. You are not free yet!

Utilize a third party. I can't emphasize this enough: If your mouth is moving, it's because you are directing people to tools and resources that tell the story efficiently and effectively. You want your most introverted friend to look back at the process you took them through and say, "I can do that"! It makes me cringe hearing a prospect that has the potential to crush it, say, "I can't do this. I'm not a salesperson.: Ugghh, they were probably puked on all over by an amateur that doesn't know when to shut the hell up!

CHAPTER 14

THEY HATE YOU

U nderstand what you are up against. Be prepared and be better. MLM hate groups are on Google, Facebook, and Reddit. If you started a hate group against any group of people, at minimum you would find big backlash against you. But that's not true for hate against MLM people! These hate groups against network marketers are run by intolerant, judgmental, ignorant hate-filled people with zero recourse and little uproar against them. These groups are filled with people feeding off each other's lack of success and too much time on their hands. A lot of them have never even been in network marketing! It's simply hate for hate's sake! I'm listening in like, "OK, you are upset because you heard from a friend of a friend that knows this guy whose sister's friend she met on a trip to Delaware failed in one of those big mean MLM companies? Did she lose her house? Her life savings? NO! They don't even know if the story is actually true. Everything is based on the fact that they heard, "People fail," "Only people at the top make money," "It's a 'pyramid scheme.'" They are usually just regurgitating something they heard from someone somewhere in the past. Here is an actual mild exchange from a Reddit group recently:

12az89 · 24d

Same. I'm not going to "support a friend" in an MLM even if the products are good. But if I can buy it in a store without the harmful side effects of a pyramid scheme...

 ⋯   ⬆ 36 ⬇

 Fomention · 24d

Agreed, but the real facts for the company are this: Some people want the product this way, and no other way.

I might buy Amway vitamins if they were on a normal shelf, but will never buy from an IBO because it would be contributing to the MLM problem.

 ⋯   ⬆ 85 ⬇

They would rather support a big company that does not give a crap about them than support a friend or (family) attempting to better themselves and bring in extra money. Huh? WTF is wrong with these people!

Now let's discuss what you will see when you Google a particular company or the industry itself. Not one review site is actually unbiased. The reviews are either from disgruntled industry failures or people who are trying to personally recruit you into that deal or another one. The biggest bait-and-switch "non-biased" review at the end pitches you to join them in Digital Real Estate! It's a game. People love to google, "Is xyz company a scam?" They then get introduced to the real scammers: the ones doing the reviews!

I could not find a single non-biased source online. Every single one is promoting something. This is important to understand. When your prospect calls to tell you they googled the company, just laugh and say, "Isn't it interesting all the BS and personal agendas online? Let's get you registered and moving toward your goals."

CHAPTER 15

I DON'T WANT TO RECRUIT FAMILY AND FRIENDS

Legit MLMs do not pay for recruiting. The interesting thing about this is there is a bad rep around this. The military pays recruiters. Professional headhunters get paid well to recruit CEOs from other companies. Colleges host recruiting days on campus. The NBA, NFL, and MLB ARE PAYING SCOUTS and agents insane money to recruit for them. The one place that actually doesn't pay people to recruit is a legit MLM. Yet that's all you hear about.

The franchise industry spends massive amounts of money on trade shows, sponsorships, and recruiters to recruit people to invest their life savings, mortgage their homes, and basically put it all on the line—time, energy, and resources.

Have you ever read the average franchise disclosure statement? Let me sum it up for you: it basically says you're an idiot if you do this. You will most likely never earn money, and if by some miracle you do get your initial investment back, you will probably still not make money.

We basically will own your dumb butt until you fold your hand. Then we have the right to resell your franchise to some other idiot.

If you had the wherewithal to purchase a big-name franchise like McDonald's, everyone would think you're a genius. However, the fact of the matter is you wouldn't get your initial investment back for five-to-seven years! You basically work for free initially. But ask someone to invest $1,000 in an MLM, where there can easily be a profit made in the first month, and everyone thinks you're a scammer.

CHAPTER 16

KNOW YOUR RATIOS

When I first started, man, I sucked! My first six months, no one joined me. Finally, my dad came on board. I think he felt sorry for me more than anything. That was enough, though, to keep me going for another six months. The energy from one person fueled me. It kept me in the game. Then usually right around the time I was ready to throw in the towel, boom, another one!

I think it's important to understand these people that joined me in the early years really didn't do much of anything. That was not important to me. The fact that someone would actually join was enough for me. Sooner or later I would find the one—the one that wants it as bad as me, the one that would do whatever it takes for as long as it takes.

In walked Poet Woods! I'll never forget it: he was suited up with a cane. He was in his early twenties, so the cane was purely for show. He walked in like he owned the place. I knew right away he and I were going to be friends. What I didn't know that day was how massive a business we would build together. I also didn't realize how many lives we were going to impact.

I should have quit long before Poet showed up, and I probably would have had I not had incredible mentors pouring into me.

"It's the ratios!" Jim Rohn said in front of a small group of us hanging on to every word this incredible man had to say. Jim taught me many things, but this, this was specifically the thing that changed everything for me.

He asked me a question. "What are your ratios?" I said, "Huh, rashooos?" He quickly caught on that I was clueless. He went on to ask, "How many people do you have to talk to, to get one to join you?" Now I was embarrassed to answer. I sucked! Like really, really bad! He threw out a number: "Twenty?" I hesitantly said, "Probably forty to fifty." To my surprise, he didn't laugh or tell me I was a loser. He said, "Great. Can you outperform someone that does 10 to 1? I immediately said no. He said, "Oh yes you can, and you will, and in the process your ratios will improve as you do the activity. You just have to do ten times the activity."

Even though it was clear this was not going to be easy, I left that day knowing I was going to beat everyone around me. I was willing to do whatever it took to change my circumstances. I mean whatever it took. If all I had to do was talk to more people, well that's exactly what I was going to do.

It didn't take long for me to start getting recognized as a top customer-getter. Not long after that, top recruiter. However, something else was happening that exploded my results. I was getting better, my ratios were improving. I kept doing the same activity with better outcomes. I was winning awards, getting recognized, and being asked to share my secrets on stages around the country. Secrets! I didn't have any! I was almost embarrassed to say it. I was just talking to everyone! I asked everyone for referrals whether they joined or not. I did this with every minute I had available to me every day that I could. I just did the same boring thing over and over and over again until someone said yes. I then taught them to do the exact same thing over and over again.

I now had the ratios down, and I started to teach the formula. I'm going to teach it to you. It's called:

650 to Freedom

Every 13 presentations = 1 new brand ambassador

Every 10 brand ambassadors = 1 leader

5 leaders = financial freedom!

Do the math. How many presentations did I have to do to get one leader? Yes, 130! Five leaders would require approximately 650 presentations. Once I understood the game. It was simply a matter of time. I could not, would not quit until I went through the numbers.

What if I built the business like most people, haphazardly making exposures from time to time, showing up when it was convenient, being inconsistent, being completely clueless, and so on. I would have quit! However, once I understood three things, it was then 100 percent on me. #1, I would have to talk to people. #2, If I talked to enough people, it was inevitable: someone would join me! #3, I would get better in the process; therefore, my numbers would continue to improve. That's exactly what I did. Went on to make tens of millions in personal commissions.

CHAPTER 17

MLM HAS A PUBLICITY PROBLEM (DON'T MAKE IT WORSE)

Unfortunately the very distributors that want to make the most money are usually contributing to the image problem. We look like clowns! One day we are screaming at the top of our lungs how we have the best thing since sliced bread. Then a few months later we are talking shit about that same company we said was our savior. Next month we are screaming at the top of our lungs about the new company that's really honest to God the one! What do you think an outside observer is thinking? Exactly! "What a bunch of immature, unprofessional idiots!"

Another thing to understand is this: People are more distracted than ever before. They have families, friends, TV, social media, holidays, parties, and a hundred other opportunities vying for their time and money. Understand what you're really up against. You have to show them this is the best use of those precious resources.

Show them that **YOU** are a committed, capable, and trustworthy leader. They are buying into you first. Take their success as seriously if not more so than your own. Do what you say. Have a real, simple, duplicatable system that you can teach. Then do it till you get the job done.

If you choose to do this and do it well, understand it is hard work. It will test and stress you. It will also stretch and grow you. The sacrifice is worth the reward.

I hope you utilize this book as a guide on your journey to building a network marketing empire. The truth is, this industry literally saved my life, and one of the best parts of it for me is the opportunity to work with and mentor both aspiring and existing entrepreneurs to build a business that gives them fulfillment, security, freedom, and so much more!

The Anti-MLM Network Marketer mentality is all about breaking the stigma around our incredible profession and truly giving you the coaching and tools to build duplicatable success throughout your organization without pummeling your friends and family with scripted messages, empty offers, unbelievable hype, archaic recruiting, and sales techniques that are not scalable.

Whenever in doubt fall back on the truth. You will do just fine.

For more resources, tools, and help, be sure to find me on social media. I've got a lot more where this came from!

SOCIAL MEDIA AND WEBSITE

Instagram: @john.malott ✓

Facebook: John Malott ✓

TikTok: @john.malott ✓

Website: johnmalott.com

Made in the USA
Columbia, SC
26 October 2023

25017298R00057